THE PASTOR'S RIB
AND HIS FLOCK

The Pastor's Rib and His Flock

by
Phyllis E. Stennett Carter

VANTAGE PRESS
New York   Washington   Hollywood

SECOND EDITION

Copyright © 1979 by Phyllis E. Stennett Carter

Published by Vantage Press, Inc.
516 West 34th Street, New York, New York 10001

Manufactured in the United States of America
Standard Book Number 533-03862-6

Library of Congress Catalog Card Number 78-60347

To my mother

I dedicate this book to the greatest woman in my life, my mother, Rosetta Stennett. A woman of rare quality, she made the most significant contribution of all by equipping me with the basic foundation and tools to face life with all of its complexities and adversities.

She generated God's love in her total outlook on life, as she projected an unwavering portion of patience that withstood mountainous trials. She ultimately overcame each test with the help of God, never complaining, but always encouraging, though at the time she needed encouragement.

Most significant of all, she was instrumental in introducing me to my Savior, the Lord Jesus Christ, who makes the difference in my life today.

I also dedicate this book to my husband, Pastor Carter, and my four lovely girls, Tracy Lorette, Tanya Lynette, Tina Louise, and Tammy Lenore.

A memorial dedication to my eldest and dearest brother, Roland Stennett. Passed May 20, 1978.

CONTENTS

Foreword

Preface

1. Needs—Spiritual, Psychological,
   Emotional   1
2. On Being Christian and Human   10
3. Your Body Is Not Your Own   17
4. Your Children   20
5. Role Conflict   25
6. Diplomacy   30
7. Broken Ribs   33
8. Educational and Social Goals   36
9. Personal Experiences   40
10. Questions Asked by Ministers' Wives   46
11. Epilogue   52
    Appendix: *The Pastor's Rib and His Flock*
    —A Teaching Guide for a Seminar
    for Pastors' and Ministers' Wives   55

FOREWORD

The word *efficacious* means "that which gets results." Our works are our efforts in a particular direction. In the panoramic view of history, we find a conspicuous presence of the "weaker" sex coming through time after time to save the day. What would have happened if Miriam had not followed the basket floating on the Nile containing her baby brother Moses? Had Deborah not agreed to go up to the battle, Barak would not have gone and disaster would have been inevitable. Had Esther not gone unheeded before the king, at the peril of losing her life, her entire nation would have been destroyed. If Bath Sheba had not interceded with the dying King David in behalf of her son Solomon, he might not have been king and soon to be regarded as the wisest man the earth has ever known. We could also mention Mary, Martha, Mary Magdalene, Dorcas, Priscilla, Lois, Eunice, and the quiet contributions they made in the furtherance of the Gospel.

Today, an effort is being made by a group of spirit-filled, consecrated, dedicated, and concerned women to inspire and incite spiritual awareness in the minds and hearts of women of God. I am proud to see how the Lord is blessing these women, inspiring them and showing them not only what to do, but how to do it. The results have been and will continue to be fantastic as long as they stay in touch with God. The test of every pudding is how it tastes.

The test of every work is the extent of the eventual results. In view of the sexual plight confronting our generation,

God has had to raise up women—attractive, intelligent, spiritual, godly, feminine, and altogether lovely women—to set the example of feminine beauty in order to offset the onslaught of homosexuality that threatens the fibers of society. My wife, Phyllis, is one of the feminine vessels God is using. She is beautiful, intelligent, strong, vibrant, enthusiastic, determined and willing to be used by God. As her husband, I think it is important to say that she is 100% woman, who never lets her writing, lecturing, and planning the various seminars interfere with her original and most important role as mother and wife. Our house is clean, the laundry is kept up, dinner is hot and ready every night, and our four girls are well mannered and obedient. Phyllis works at a full-time job as an executive secretary at Pfizer Chemical. She is president of the women's auxiliary at our local church, and she shares in my duties of counseling the youth in our church. She is constantly invited to lecture women's groups in other churches. If you do not get the point, I will say it in plain English, my wife is fantastic.

Complement a good leader with good support, and you have good results. But Phyl has an outstanding team that works hand-in-hand with each other. I see their function as tremendously important and sorely needed. So many women are not aware of, and therefore unprepared to fill, the roles and provide the services God intended for women.

Every woman cannot cope with the pressures of the ministry, and therefore, should not be a minister's wife. Every woman cannot understand the treachery and devastating capacity of Satan. They should not lead.

The works of this group of soldiers will eventually bear measurable fruit. Fruit in the ranks of women throughout Christendom performed by the Women's Christian World is indeed efficacious. Although the Christian woman is their primary target, Christian men will also reap the fruitful benefits.

Pastor R. H. Carter

PREFACE

Being a pastor's wife is more than a notion; it is the kind of position that is not desired, chosen, or selected by the woman. She can make or break her man. She can determine failure or success for his pastorate. Many are called, but few are capable or willing. She is prepared and developed through mountainous trials until God forms her into the vessel called helpmate. Pride must be swallowed, tears must be shed, many things must be left unsaid. She must be satisfied to dwell in the shadow of her husband, walking just behind. She must be able to help him with a subtle push, never an obvious shove; a passing suggestion, never a blaring command. She must be there when she's needed most to help, to listen, to understand and share. A pastor's wife must be insensitive, but yet sensitive to everyone's needs. It can be a rewarding position if she can learn to wait. The secret is in learning how to wait. She must love people, and learn to respect young and old. She must sacrifice her time and her needs for the needs of others. She must share her husband's burdens. She must be able to observe the moods and feeling of others in aiding the pastor. And most important, she must be able to discern when to speak and when not. (Most of the time she will not speak.) She must be aware of the close tie between her and the congregation, and be able to cite each situation in the church as a learning experience in effectively dealing with people of all classes.

May be able to comprehend with all saints what is the breadth, and length, and depth, and height; and to know the love of Christ, which passeth knowledge, that ye might be filled with all the fullness of God. (Ephesians 3:18-19)

The pastor's wife is in the spotlight, viewed by an audience whose members are from various backgrounds and social status. Her performance is rated with scrupulous exactitude. She is expected to achieve "*their*" goals. However, as she learns, she must constantly look to God, not at what the congregation expects of her, or what society feels she should be. Her one single purpose and aim is God's "Well Done" rating.

Being a pastor's wife is not always negative and imposing; it has its privileges and advantages. Most significant, such a wife can share in the blessing of being her husband's core support and prayer partner as he effectively propagates the Word of God. The life of the pastor's wife is developed through preparatory stages, enabling her to observe, scrutinize, reflect, and accept situations and conditions so that she is able to encourage someone else traveling the same road. How can members be aided unless the pastor's wife can relate through her own experiences. She can be either an asset or a liability to her husband's ministry. In my short period as a pastor's wife (fourteen years), I must say with all sincerity that sometimes I would like to do as I please for a change of pace and not worry about offending anyone; but I must remember that if I behave thus, it will reflect upon the pastor. The most significant lesson I've learned is to be satisfied with myself as an individual, and to be sure that God is pleased with my motives and objectives as I seek the perfect will of God. This can only be done through prayer, fasting, and trusting in the Lord. The title of this book, *The Pastor's Rib and His Flock*, is intended to be thought-provoking, stimulating, and reflective of the challenge of the pastoral ministry. A pastor's wife does not enjoy an ideal life because she is stereotyped by her peers, the congregation, and society.

She must learn to allow God to be her constant companion and develop through a prayerful life a total dependency on God for help in all of her decisions.

The effectual fervent prayer of a righteous man availeth much. (James 5:16)

My husband has been pastoring for twenty-three years and has founded two churches. Before accepting Christ, he was a talented jazz musician, proficient in seven instruments.

He started pastoring at age twenty-seven (I was twenty-four). He attended Bible college in the evenings for eight years, finally receiving his Bachelor's and Master's degrees in Theology. Both my husband and I worked daily; I stopped in between to have my children, and then went back to work. God always supplied the baby sitters. We now have four lovely girls, ranging from eighteen to twenty-four years of age and a granddaughter, age two; this gives you a clear picture of God's maneuvering on our behalf. I am not going to say that it has been easy. Things were rough but having "God" and "Love," on our side gave us a double determination to continue for the cause of Christ. "For greater love hath no man than this, that a man lay down his life for his friends." (John 15:12-13).

A pastor's wife is automatically in a category of her own. No one understands but another pastor's wife.

What prompted and stimulated my desire to write this book, was the mere fact that I became more and more aware of the importance of being prepared for this task. This preparation is especially important for the young ministerial wives. Their primary purposes in life are to aid their husbands spiritually, psychologically, and emotionally; to know the importance of their place as a minister's wife and to excel to whatever height God designs for them; and to deal with relevant issues that such young wives are confronted with, such as: Age limitations, if any; Personal convictions vs. biblical and scriptural restrictions; and Individuality—being your real self (don't pattern yourself after manmade models).

It was a step-by-step process for me, not having my prior teaching in this area. However, God guided my every footstep. He took me into his bosom of knowledge and granted me years of experience, physically unearned, and cushioned me with a great security in Him. That's why I love Him today for being my constant companion; I'm glad that I submitted to His will.

I would like to take this opportunity to express my gratitude to my church home, Refuge Church of Christ, Roosevelt, New York; better known as "The Roosevelt Family." I have grown to love this group very much. I thank them for the opportunity to be their pastor's wife, and although I'm not perfect, I'm certainly striving to be in God's divine will. I also pay tribute to Verona Thornton and Carol Williams, students of the Teaching Seminar for Pastors' and Ministers' Wives (a seminar that I conducted in my local church). They made it possible for me to further my experience by helping others to recognize how they struggle to become better minister's wives. They projected an overwhelming interest in striving to learn more of God's word, which made my teaching job very rewarding.

My thanks go also to Mazie LaMelle, a very dear friend and close worker who encouraged me and prayed for God's will to be done in my life. I'm grateful to Constance J. Dixon for allowing me to use her personal experience indicated in the chapter, "Your Children." Many thanks to William I. Moore, B.A., M.S.W., a field-work instructor at Fordham University, Graduate School of Social Services, who made a significant contribution to my book. Thanks also go to Dr. Robert Spellman, B.S., M.A., Ph.D., president of the Church of Our Lord Jesus Christ Bible College, who made it possible for me to conduct a weekend seminar for pastors' and ministers' wives. He gave me much constructive advice for my book. Another very dear friend, Larry Stouder, was very helpful in the preparation of my book. Thanks go to James I. Clark, Jr., Th.B., M.B.A. for his encouragement and inspiration to further the work of God.

Most of all, I would like to thank my husband, Pastor R. H. Carter, B.A., Th.B., Th.M., whose patience, love and understanding allowed me to work extensively with my book; this was indeed a sacrifice. His contribution also included his expertise in editing and pointing out critical areas for consideration.

My greatest contribution came from Bernice Chisholm, a wonderful woman of God who edited my book and supplied the title, *The Pastor's Rib and His Flock*.

God bless Debbie McCormick who did all of the manuscript typing.

THE PASTOR'S RIB
AND HIS FLOCK

1

NEEDS—SPIRITUAL, PSYCHOLOGICAL, EMOTIONAL

There is a distinct difference between the position of the young wife of a minister and the mature wife. There are emotional, psychological, and spiritual differences that vary and affect her role. If she is not made aware of what to expect in her role, whether young or mature, it can cause an *emotional disaster*, a *psychological disorder*, and a *spiritual deficiency*. All three of these aspects can affect her motivations, which in turn will influence the achievement goals, i.e., the desire to perform well and to succeed. The young wife will try harder than the mature wife to attain more success in different kinds of situations; on the other hand, the mature wife has already attained experiences which give her a cushion and a deeper sense of security. Most important, she must look to God to be her constant companion in leading and guiding her in ALL of her decisions.

The minister's wife recognizes a need to please church members; but in time, she will ultimately realize it is humanly impossible to please so many people at one time. Her only responsibility is to God and her husband. The items listed below are important for her to know:

—She is only one person

—She is only required to please God totally, and her husband within her limitations.
—Remember there is no perfect pastor's wife, because there is no perfect person.
—LOVE yourself—don't covet someone else's personality; remember you have beautiful qualities, too.

The only way you can develop a wholesome relationship with others, is by being able to deal with yourself. This, however, does not exempt the mature wife or allow her to neglect these characteristics; there are always exceptions to every rule.

DEALING WITH TENSIONS

Tensions are caused by conflict between what the congregation and her husband expect of the minister's wife, and what she wants to be and do. In addition, she must deal with her own concept of the ideal minister's wife. Ultimately, she becomes overwhelmed with feelings of inferiority because of a lack of confidence. This affects her home life and her husband's ministry.

Many things must be taken into account, such as:

—She is inexperienced and often impetuous in her role.
—In respect to decisions, she is uncertain and unsure.
—She is sensitive and vulnerable to hurt feelings.
—Because she is young, the possibility of small children and added housework, can cause emotional strain.
—She may suffer from financial insolvency.
—She may feel inferior and inadequate because she lacks a good education or is jealous of husband's extensive involvement.

The remedy may be one or more of the following:

—Develop a one-to-one relationship with God—ask Him for direction and wait patiently for His answer.
—Discipline yourself to read the Word of God, consistently.

2

—Be warm and friendly with church members, but not overly close with them.
—Know your faults and don't deceive yourself; deal with your deficiencies daily.
—Reach out for something that gives you fulfillment, geared to please God.

The pastor's young wife should be aware that:

1. Her husband not only belongs to her, but to the members.
2. They can work independent of each other, together, and/or for the same purpose.
3. Sensitivity is a luxury in her role as a pastor's wife.
4. Focusing her attention on aiding others can be a blessing.
5. She needs to encourage her husband, even though she might need encouragement.
6. Encouraging others and praying for the success of her husband's ministry makes her own problems seem minimal.

Young wives of ministers must know how to deal with all age groups, especially mature lay members. Respect and diplomacy are tools which must be sharply developed. Mature members must feel *loved, needed,* and *remembered*; so often, this age group is pushed aside and forgotten. Remember, the mature member is better equipped to help *YOU* in your role, than any other member. Her life experiences have taught lessons that in some instances, exceed those learned through formal education. However, there are exceptions to every rule. The pastor's wife cannot demand respect from church members; she must earn it. Try not to display emotional feelings in public. Learn to discipline and govern personal attitudes in a discreet, consistent, and nonpartisan fashion.

EMOTIONAL NEEDS

Excitement and passion bring on a particular reaction. Being able to control your emotions at any given time is very necessary; it is the result of discipline. You must be conditioned to the sensitivity of others and deny the luxury of your own feelings:

> —Every act you display, every word uttered *is* *"scrutinized"*;
> —Every decision made—your husband's or others—that you rebel against, is a negative attribute in your personality that must be *broken down.*

Be kindly affectioned one to another with brotherly *LOVE*, in honour preferring one another (Romans 12:10).

PSYCHOLOGICAL NEEDS

You should first deal with yourself, accepting the fact that you have insecurities that must be recognized, dealt with, and eventually disposed of. The problem stems from the fact that you do not accept what you really are. This becomes a problem to you and everyone you come in contact with. Ultimately, you become a liability to your husband's ministry. Thank God, there is a remedy for *all* who surrender completely to God's will. Oh how simple to merely say such words, but *how* hard we make the task! A. W. Tozer expresses his ideas in his pamphlet "Total Commitment to Christ":

Your total commitment to God involves:

> 1. Intellectual attachment
> 2. Volitional attachment
> 3. Exclusive attachment
> 4. Inclusive attachment
> 5. Irrevocable attachment
>
> —High mental capacity
> —Your will
> —To shut others out
> —Including everything concerned

4

—Cannot be changed

God *does* require total commitment from your lives. If you *willingly* submit to these attachments to Christ, there is nothing that God will not do for you.

> I Beseech you therefore, brethren, by the mercies of God, that ye present your bodies a living sacrifice, holy, acceptable unto God, which is your reasonable service. And be not conformed to this world: but be ye transformed by the renewing of your mind, that ye may prove what is that good, and acceptable, and perfect, will of God (Romans 12:1-2).

You cannot have a wholesome relationship with others until you have an adequate view of yourself. You must be able to face life with all its tears, pain, and injustice, and still possess joy and hope. To be able to obtain a positive outlook on life, "you must be able to create happiness in your own life before you can give it."

> For God hath not given us the spirit of fear; but of power, and of love, and of a sound mind (II Timothy 1:7).

Create a positive oneness involving you and your husband with problems, crises, and misunderstandings. If you already have it, develop it; if you don't, work at it. Use your ingenuity; dream it, do anything, as long as you get it! It is your foundation for a happy home. It is his foundation for a well-rounded ministry and for its growth. It is also the basis for you to develop your unique personality, molded into God's image for you.

SPIRITUAL NEEDS

> For they that are after the flesh do mind the things of the flesh; but they that are after the spirit, the things of

5

the spirit. For to be carnally minded is death; but to be spiritually minded is life and peace (Romans 5,6,8:14).

For as many as are led by the spirit of God, they are the sons of God. To be spiritually minded you must follow these three steps:

1. Totally commit yourself to Christ
2. Separate yourself from the world.
3. Be transformed by the renewing of your mind (see Romans 12:2).

There must be a constant renewing of the mind—a daily inner renewal of your spiritual frame—for the mind is continually refreshed by meditating on the things pertaining to God. Table 1, below, will be helpful in this regard:

TABLE 1
HOW TO DEVELOP A DEEPER SENSE OF SPIRITUAL AWARENESS

Mark of Stewardship	Romans 8:14
Mark of Spiritual Bankruptcy	Revelation 3:17
Spiritual Awareness	I Corinthians 2:10-16
OPERATIONAL DEFINITION:	To be sensitive and responsive to the moving, direction, works, and will of God via the unctions of the Holy Spirit (I John 2:20).
SPIRIT INDWELLING	Ezekiel 36:27; John 14:17; Romans 8:9; I Corinthians 6:19,20; I John 2:27
PROCESS OF DEVELOPMENT	Romans 5:1-5
SPIRITUAL VERIFICATION	Romans 8:16; Galatians 4:6; I John 3:24; I John 4:13

Spiritual Development is the result of *Prayer, Bible Study,* and *Fasting.* The most important of these is *prayer,* which is the direct and uninhibited process of communication with *God Himself.* Prayer is a dialogue between lovers. If you don't talk to God, and are not familiar with the sound of his voice, you are not praying enough, or at all; this is no one's fault but yours (John 10:27). Prayer is a conversation, request, petition, plea or intercession of a person directed to *God.* It is not an exercise to outyell, outmoan, outgroan each other. It is not a speech using memorized phrases of pious rhymes, or spiritualized metaphors we've heard someone else use. *It is the sincere desire of the heart.* The person who learns how to pray successfully, learns how to give *God* His turn to talk. If we believe God for an answer, we must learn how to wait on the answer. Why are we so impotent and fruitless today, compared to the first-century Saints? The answer is to be found in one word, unbelief. No one word so describes the spirit of the average Christian as does the word *unbelief.* The Lord Jesus Christ has commissioned us to go and share the good news of the gospel everywhere, but we huddle in disbelief in our little prayer meetings (those who go to prayer meetings) and talk of peripheral superficial matters. We are content to see accomplished in the name of Christ only that which man is capable of accomplishing through his own intellect, eloquence, and organizational ability. Instead of calling upon the mighty power of God and believing God for the supernatural happening to come about, we go aimlessly on our own way, impotent, unbelieving, fruitless, and aware of any and everything but the Holy Spirit. If we get together and pray, not only will there be an impact on each of us but *we will shake up this whole place* (Acts 4:24-30).

All mankind instinctively prays, even to false gods built of sticks and stones. Whenever he is faced with tragedy, heartache, sorrow or danger, he prays. There is a serious danger in this ignorant prayer. It is a well established fact of philosophy and history that man always assimilates the character of the object he worships. People who have worshipped gods of lust have become morally degenerate. When men have prayed to gods of blood, fire, and war, they have become militaristic, ruthless, and sadistic. This same principle applies to the child of God. As we behold His face, we are changed into His image. We should pray always by developing an *attitude of prayer.* First of all, pray that your inner man may be renewed and quickened; be made alive, alert, vital, refreshed, sensitive to and empowered by the Holy Spirit. Pray about your problems; pray for wisdom and guidance, for strength to resist temptation, for comfort in time of sorrow. Pray for everything—there is nothing too small or too great to bring before the Lord. Prayer makes you sensitive to the Holy Spirit's bidding. Seek to maintain an attitude of prayer wherever you are, and in all you do. Always have a private, personal, secret place where you can hide away with God. Spend some time with Him each day. Make intercession daily for your loved ones, friends, neighbors, co-workers, government leaders, pastor, and even for those who despitefully use you, using the guidelines indicated in Table 2.

TABLE 2
REQUISITES TO ANSWERED PRAYER

Ask believing	Matthew 21:22
Ask in Jesus' Name	John 14:14
Clean Heart	Psalms 66:18
Forgiving Spirit	Mark 11:25
Pray in Faith	Matthew 9:29
Pray to glorify God	John 14:13
Directions to Pray	I Thessalonians 5:17; Matthew 26:41; Phillippians 4:6; I Corinthians 14:15; Luke 18:1; I Timothy 2:1,2; Ephesians 6:19
Prayer is God's delight	Proverbs 15:8

To try to live a spiritual life without praying is like trying to lead a natural life without breathing. It just cannot be done! And so how do you develop a deeper sense of spiritual awareness? Pray about it.

Bible study focuses on the *Word* of God which reveals the *Will* of God. You must have the information available in the Word of God. In order to assuredly know and do the right thing, you have to know what it is; you must also have some idea of what the wrong thing is about. All of this information is in God's words (II Timothy 2:15).

The significance of *Fasting* is twofold: It is a sacrifice and God honors and responds to all sacrifices, great or small. Second, and most important, it is the best procedure you can use to develop personal discipline. If you can withstand the pangs of self-induced hunger, the result of your election not to eat, then you can withstand a great deal of things for God. The first law of nature is self-preservation; the first law of *God* is self-denial.

2

ON BEING CHRISTIAN AND HUMAN

As there was on the desk of President Harry S. Truman, supposedly there is now on the desk of President Jimmy Earl Carter, a sign that reads, "The Buck Stops Here." In the community of the church, that particular slogan is applicable to each and every pastor; it is expected, it is respected. Leadership is compensated with reverence and respect. Nobody, however, takes into consideration the assistants and lieutenants who make every good administration work. No one considers the support that every leader must have. Very little praise is directed toward the burden-bearers, and heavy-load-sharers who faithfully carry out the details and menial tasks necessary to make every program work. In this unsung throng dwells the pastor's wife. She is the most criticized and scrutinized individual in each and every church. Her children are watched with scrupulous exactitude. Her house is examined with a fine-tooth comb for cleanliness, and her clothing is compared with the most archaic and most outlandish styling. Her speech is expected to be perfect, and so is her temper.

Being Christian, human, and a pastor's wife is very difficult. First of all, by virtue of being so very close to the pastor, she must share almost all of his burdens whether or not she knows the exact details of the problems. She must shore

10

up her husband's drooping shoulders and encourage him through crisis after crisis, so that he may encourage others. She must be the most discreet, most diplomatic woman in the church. Everyone else can have a good idea or program, and be willing to fight for it at business meetings or committee caucuses, but if the pastor's wife tries to explain a situation she feels is right, then not only is she pushy, *but* overbearing and domineering. On the other hand, if a woman is a good helpmate, a supporter, a backstop for her husband's problems, then she is equated with strength—a tower of strength that is ever ready with a comforting word for everyone else, and an unfailing source of help. But what happens when the pastor's Mrs. gets tired, or when she has problems? It is true that a prophet is often without honor in his own land, and many times the woman is without pity and understanding in her own home.

Being Christian and human affords each one of us the opportunity to realize that although we are spirit-filled, we are not perfect. Every woman who is married in the church has two husbands: her husband and her pastor. Every single woman has her pastor to be her husband when she needs masculine support. Many times the pastor's wife must share her husband so much that she finds herself without a husband at all, that is, except when he needs *her*. Why isn't he available when she needs *him*? No woman can understand this burden unless she is a pastor's wife. Not even a minister's wife understands because the responsibilities and expectations are different.

Praise is needed and cherished by everyone, and criticism should be expected and accepted, especially if it is constructive. However, when one is criticized *all* the time, and there is never any praise coming, not even when a person does well, then it is just not fair. Being Christian and human makes you realize that, without that good woman, that good man could very well be a complete flop and a total failure! Being Christian and human makes you accept one another for what you are, and instead of analyzing each other critically, leads you to

11

offer prayer for the breakdowns and shortcomings in each other.

People will give their pastor almost anything, but their pastor's wife get absolutely nothing. Regretfully the problems discussed above are almost universal. Until the members of the church community realize that helping their pastor's wife is, in essence, helping their pastor, then this travesty of justice will continue.

Finally, I feel many times it is the pastor who gives the people the misconceived idea that he is "super"; the only one who is "super" is *Jesus*. If the pastor does not praise and support his own wife from the pulpit, he cannot expect the people to accept her. Their appreciation of her will not be any higher than his expressed evaluation.

There are some Christians who have progressed in Christ to the extent of reaching first base; some are rounding second; some are rounding third, and almost home; others are just getting up to bat. But not one has crossed home plate. Only Jesus has reached the pinnacle of perfection.

Let us understand one another, and we will better demonstrate the much needed love that we have to each other. This is the first commandment, the new commandment, and the old commandment combined in one. Being Christian and human is to be full of love and understanding for one and for all.

With this in mind, look at Table 3, which shows how a pastor's wife can help him build his ministry. To do this, however, the wife *must* be able to fight off the effects of depression, loneliness, guilt, and self-pity better than most other people.

TABLE 3
HOW A PASTOR'S WIFE CAN HELP HER HUSBAND
BUILD A MEANINGFUL, GROWING, AND DYNAMIC MINISTRY

1. Love for the Lord
2. Love for the ministry (see Ephesians 4:11-12 and Colossians 4:17)
3. Love for the people (see Romans 3:10)
4. Mental acceptance that your husband belongs to the people.

5. Willing to sacrifice and share YOUR time with others.
6. Willing to share your HUSBAND in moments of need.
7. Recognize that every positive part you play adds tremendous dimension to the ministry.
8. Recognize that the ministry is more important than YOU.
9. The pastor's wife must fit into her husband's plans, YES, it means you have married his profession and, YES, you may have him only on a part time basis.
10. Believe and have faith that prayer changes all things.
11. "Wait on the Lord, be of good courage and he shall strengthen thine heart" (Psalms 27:14).

OVERCOMING DEPRESSION

Depression leads to low spiritual morale, so that we become vulnerable to Satan's trickery. Remember what the apostle Peter advised the early Christians? He told them to cast all their cares upon the Lord, and assured them of God's ever continuing care.

For God hath not given us the spirit of fear; but of *Power* and of *Love,* and of a Sound *Mind* (II Tim. 1:7).

Thou wilt keep him in perfect peace WHOSE mind is stayed on thee, because he trusteth in thee (Isaiah 26:3).

Knowing this, that the trying of your faith worketh patience. But let patience have her PERFECT WORK, that ye may be perfect and entire, wanting nothing (James 1:3-4).

OVERCOMING LONELINESS

The pastor's wife becomes alienated simply because no one but another pastor's wife understands her life. Loneliness leads to ineffective service. Loneliness is universal and is common to all, and it is a condition that comes in many different forms:

—It hides behind sorrow.
—It cringes when it feels ignored.
—It yields to molds of despondency.
—It fancies itself unloved and unappreciated.
—It longs for familiar cries.

Here are some ways to deal with loneliness:

—Seek other outlets—your own ministry;
—Use your hidden talents to do an effective work for God, one that gives you satisfaction and spiritual gratification;
—Recognize that you have a greater ministry, *the Ministry of "the Interior"*—i.e., providing for your husband's physical needs (For instance, by providing attractive, nourishing, well balanced meals) and administering to his emotional needs.

OVERCOMING SELF-PITY

Self-pity leads to:

—Constant complaining
—Griping
—Unhappy personality
—Negative outlook

Self-pity ensues because of the demand placed upon your symbolic role. Even though stress and strain are great, the pastor's wife's plight is an honorable one and can be a great one. She must be able to maintain a positive outlook on life and to create happiness in her own life; only then can she give it.

A virtuous woman is a crown to her husband: but she that maketh ashamed is as rottenness in his bones (Proverbs 12:4).

Believe it or not, there are joys and privileges in being a pastor's wife. One of the greatest joys is seeing a response to the Word of God and the change in the lives of the people to whom you and your husband minister.

I'm glad that I'm a pastor's wife,
I truly count it joy
To daily walk and work with one
Who is in God's employ.

True, I sometimes feel resentment
That my time is seldom mine,
When I begrudge the time to pray,
"Lord, I would be fully thine,"

Though I know the deep frustration
Of my housework never done,
Of seldom having time to read
Or doing things "just for Fun."

I do not know the boredom
Of empty, aimless days,
So though I'm often weary,
My heart is filled with praise.

Should we not count it joy to bear
The burden of another?
Then I blush with shame and whisper,
With needy youth or mother?

Is there not sweet satisfaction
In watching children grow
Into Christian youth and then go out
The gospel seed to sow?

So though my time is seldom mine,
The phone and doorbell ring,
I'm glad that I'm a pastor's wife,
It makes me want to sing.

Marian Van Dam

OVERCOMING GUILT

There are many forms of guilt, and one is brought on by your worse enemy, your own personal approval of yourself. A peak of intensity and self-condemnation attacks the human mind, causing additional stress. There is another type of guilt which is more damaging because it stunts your spiritual growth—self-blame and personal hatred.

What Causes Guilt Feelings?

1. Guilt is felt when one fails to attain his own high expectations. You torment yourself because you set high standards and unreasonable goals.
2. Trying to live up to someone else's expectations.
3. Problems and temptations common to human nature.

Remember this *famous expression*: "It is *human* to err but *divine* to forgive."

3

YOUR BODY IS NOT YOUR OWN

What? know ye not that your body is the temple of the Holy Ghost which is in you, which you have of God, and ye are not your own? For ye are bought with a price, therefore glorify God in your body, and in your spirit, which are God's (I Corinthians 6:19).

If your body is the temple of the Holy Ghost, you should do all you can to preserve, nourish, and strengthen it to be a vessel of honor. When you begin to misuse your body, you inhibit the work of God. People tend to put so much emphasis upon their attire: how long the dress, how dark the color, how sad the face. This is suppose to be the badge of humility to those who do not realize that humility comes from within. You completely forget about what goes into the body, and life then becomes unbalanced, unfruitful, unseasoned, and unproductive.

The following limitations will give you an introspection into the inner man.

—If you eat pork or highly seasoned foods when you know you have high-blood pressure, you are tempting God.

—Don't blame the devil when you overindulge and inflict sickness upon your body. (Poor Satan, he gets

17

blamed for more than he deserves.)

—If there is nothing else to do, don't eat. Eating is just a habit. The devil will give you a habit and enslave you. Frustration, in many cases, causes excess eating.

When you inflict punishment on yourself, you create mental anxiety. Ultimately, your friends begin to wonder what kind of God you are serving because you are always in a state of turmoil, unhappiness, and insecurity.

Two beautiful scriptures come to mind. One says: "Thou wilt keep him in perfect peace, whose mind is stayed on thee because he trusteth in thee. (Isaiah 26:3). The secret in this scripture is that peace can come only to the individual whose mind is on the Lord. When your mind becomes stimulated by other things (carnality, materialism), you automatically remove yourself from the will of God. Therefore, you become vulnerable to Satan, losing out with God.

The other scripture says: "Let not then your good be evil spoken of." (Romans 14:16). Many times you tend to express Christ in your outward appearance (clothes) but, you exhibit fear, anxiety, and everything that is unlike God in the inward man. The Word of God tells us (in Romans 12:10) to be temperate in all things; that includes food.

When you run your body down, working two jobs and doing other things, your body screams out for help. You are obviously too tired to worship the Lord. This is no asset to your husband's ministry. You can only do an effective work for God when you submit your body in the complete state for His ultimate glorification. God requires that you present your body a living sacrifice, holy and acceptable unto God, which is your reasonable service.

It becomes inconceivable and impossible to ever comply to His will when your body is a total wreck and your mind is wandering aimlessly. The Holy Spirit does not act unseemly, but He is a God of order. You claim to be used of God all hours of the night and you have jobs to go to the next day, yet your body is screaming, "help."

Your mental faculties get washed out under such strain

18

and you look like something the cat dragged in. You cannot exemplify Christ under these circumstances; you are certainly an embarrassment to God! Dr. Marion H. Nelson, Christian psychiatrist and author, stated:

> To continue to study after the mind is exhausted is to abuse it. The Holy Spirit usually does not lead a Christian to do that which is abusive to his mind or body. The Christian should stop and go to bed, so that the next day, his mind will be rested and will be responsive to God's directions.

Your body is the facility through which you are in complete control. It is the body that responds to a given desire, depending upon the shape your body is in. It is also the body that functions spontaneously either spiritually or carnally, depending upon your strengths or your area of commitment. If you recognize the importance of your body, your service and worship to God will be placed on a higher priority level.

4

YOUR CHILDREN

In christendom, there are problems that are faced by the ministerial couple that demand sacrifices by the entire family. Your children are an intricate part of your family unit and require special attention and consideration. Unless you comply with your maternal responsibility and your responsibility to God, your worship to God becomes of no effect. See I Tim. 5:8.

The wife must be the one to generate that "adhesive quality" that brings about unity among all component parts of the family structure—husband, wife and children—all in God's divine order.

> But I would have you know, that the head of the woman is the man; and the head of Christ is God" (I Corinthians 11:3).

The ministerial family has many roles that can indeed cause conflicts, when there is an effort to please every one involved: wife, children, and church members. Your husband's time is devoted to the service of the people. He is preoccupied with (1) new dimensions in his ministry, (2) developing a prayerful life, and (3) administering to the people's spiritual and material needs. Finally, he is pressured by the wife and the children, who express legitimate feelings of abandonment.

As the wife of a minister, many times you are the last one on the list for attention and consideration.

However, your children are the most intricate part of the family unit, and the parents should recognize the pressures and problems faced by them. Children are sensitive, open, and uninhibited. Unless they receive proper attention, understanding, and guidance from both father and mother, problems will develop and grow out of proportion. It is quite important to give as much time as possible to your children, to reassure them of your love. It is your responsibility as spiritual parents and leaders to effectively guide your children in fulfilling their basic needs; a deep sense of security, recognition, achievement, respect, dignity, and good self-image. When you fail to comply with this responsibility, you are serving God in part only.

Professor Howard Hendricks in his book, *Heaven Help The Home*, says:

> Provide your child's basic needs, not all his wants or your frustrated desires for him, but his needs. Privacy, a place to play and study, clean clothes, ownership of his own things, time to be alone, a sensible program of eating and exercise, opportunity to make appropriate decisions and always tell him the truth.

Following these basic rules for regulating a home life for your children should result in a balanced home life centered around God.

Down through the years, society has stereotyped ministers' children as "the Pastor's bad kid." This opinion however, has no validity or real significance to justify it.

I spoke to a ministerial couple whose family life example refutes this statement. Their living testimony is proof that the ministerial family can indeed have a normal, fruitful, and productive home life with respect to its attitudes in and out of the church and its dealing with society. This couple's "better half" indicated to me that her main ingredient is love, followed by a combination of faith, trust, and hope. Through the

21

years, her family members have built their life to trust each member, including the youngest sibling. Constance J. Dixon also stated that prayer was the basic tool used in their daily family life. Each situation in the home, from a toothache to the need of finances for bills, is taken to God in prayer. The foundation and existence of their entire life, has been and still is, "prayer."

> The effectual fervent prayer of a righteous man availeth much (James 5:16).

There is a role for each member of the family which satisfies psychological needs and the urge for self-esteem. Each family member has developed a beautiful rapport with each other, and together, with God. It is a blessing that they allowed prayer to be the nucleus of their lives. The family that projects these traits will undoubtedly avoid the gap of which many parents are guilty.

There are so many distractions outside of the home that can indeed affect the child: peer group pressure, affection, prestige. Therefore, ministerial parents should cultivate their children through daily devotion in the home and, most important, by serving as living examples to be patterned after. In light of this challenge, you must be spiritual leaders and take a stand in the proper development and spiritual growth of your child. Consider these three basic steps:

1. *Family Devotion* Be sure to set a scheduled time for each gathering.
2. *Family Recreation* Develop some type of recreation that the family can enjoy together.
3. *Family Counsel* Build a parent-child relationship. Respect the child's views, whether or not you believe them. It becomes quite important to the child that you listen instead of criticize.

It is often said that the ministerial couple becomes such a blessing to others in solving problems for everyone else, that it is blind to its own problematical situations at home. This, of course, engenders a feeling of neglect, of being unloved, and widens the gulf of communication within the family unit.

The fact that I am the mother of four girls, that I work and attend college (not to mention the church activities I participate in) have caused me to reevaluate my priorities. I have recognized the importance of family togetherness, and tried to implement various means of creating a cohesive and stimulating relationship within our household. At least once a week, I prepare a large breakfast (preferably on Saturday) for the family around the dining-room table. We discuss school problems, if any, and try to relate to whatever is important to the children. What is even more effective is dining out for breakfast. This provides the privacy the children need to share with both mother and father. Dining out eliminates the phone and door bell interruptions that usually attend you at home. This, of course, must be worked at to meet your family's needs. Initially, it is a struggle because of the stringent schedule in which both pastor and wife are involved. But as you recognize the ultimate benefit, a genuine effort will prove to be effective.

I cite the following situation because it warrants special attention, particularly for those in similar circumstances. It gives you an indication of family struggles and sacrifices. I had a conversation with a Christian friend whose father is bishop of a large congregation and has been the pastor of their church for as long as she can remember. Her family consists of fifteen children: six boys and nine girls. This friend approached me and asked quite candidly: "Does God require such devoted service from a man of God, when he must leave home to start other missions to the extent that his own home and family are neglected?" She felt that her father should have been able to serve God and still fulfill his family responsibilities by being home when he was needed for counsel, guidance, instruction, and, most of all, to engender a healthy male and father image.

The children felt that, because of their father, undue

hardships were inflicted upon a family as large as theirs. Many questions were left unanswered. Many crises were handled poorly because their father who was a help to so many others, was never available to tend to the needs and hurts of his own family. He had time to work for God's family throughout the world but neglected the work for God's family at home. This unfortunately resulted in a waning of love within the family and irreparable damage.

Occasionally, it becomes necessary for spiritual leaders to reevaluate their priorities in order to effectively keep their home life and worship to God in proper perspective. Being saved for many years, this friend referred to above, questioned the validity of her father's worship and service to God when it resulted in family disaster.

I have certainly taken inventory of my priorities, praying each day for the Lord to take control of my mind. But in order for that to happen, I must allow the Lord to have his way in my life. In effect, I am saying, "Lord, not my will—but thy will be done." The pastor's wife must recognize that her husband's responsibility to his flock is very demanding, and that it often requires frequent absences from the home. On the other hand, she must be wise and creative enough to plan and conserve each moment afforded the family as precious moments that are vital to the entire family unit.

5

ROLE CONFLICT

In our changing society, emphasis is placed upon "Role Conflict." This has caused dissension for the ministerial couple when the wife out of necessity or the need for fulfillment seeks employment. Priorities must have preeminence when the minister's wife fails to produce spiritually and hinders the work of God. It, therefore, becomes essential to consult God to discover His perfect will. It is not enough to be in His submissive will, but to be in His divine will; that is where we all should strive to be.

Our women years ago were placed in a strict category: docile; subservient; meek; always ready, willing and able to serve the male image in every way. It was her way of life, it was all she knew. Her job was the home: cooking, cleaning, and rearing the children. In essence, her role was that of a servant. However, we thank God, for time certainly changes all things. Our men are faced with the threat of equality. In many instances, women are forced to work to help supplement their husband's salary and make ends meet. Many newly acquired positions have been won for females, which have given them dignity and respect. Their economic status has increased substantially; a sense of challenge, accomplishment, and achievement now adds significant dimensions to the woman's role.

With her new-found status, the wife is faced with role

conflict, which imposes upon her home duties. She must reconcile her duties as a lay wife and a minister's wife. If children are involved, the demands are increased and must be met.

Horton and Hunt, noted sociologists, describe the two kinds of role conflicts as follows:

> There are at least two kinds of role conflicts: conflicts between roles, and conflicts within a single role. Often two or more roles (either independent roles or parts of a role set) may impose conflicting obligations upon a person. The employed wife finds that the demands of her job may conflict with home duties; the married student must reconcile student role demands with duties as husband or wife; the police officer must sometimes choose between violating his duty and arresting a friend. Or, within a single role, there may be a structured (built-in) conflict. Very few roles are completely free from structured role conflicts.

It is not surprising that when children have become independent and mother is stirred to "do something," she is psychologically immobilized. She has never been attuned to her own individualistic style of functioning. She is so used to functioning for others that she has immense guilt to overcome before she can feel free to spend time on herself. Women never reach their full potential unless they start to function as individuals within the marriage relationship. They must continue to develop if they are to find personal happiness and be of some good to others.

Because of modern technology, the woman of today is free from traditional drudgeries and has more leisure time than her grandmother, and because of this, increasing numbers of females are returning to work. Women are hoping to fulfill themselves and find the answer to the problem of their middle years. According to Duvall, a noted sociologist, nineteenth-century mothers were totally consumed with their homes and children, so practically half never entered paid employment. Today, nine out of ten women are employed in the course of their lives, and three out of every ten are married. In fact, a government pamphlet published in 1969 showed that three out of every five women in the labor force were thirty-five or over. This same study indicated that nearly sixty percent were married and living with their husbands. This would therefore suggest that the majority of women work, not out of economic necessity but, rather to raise their standards of living and to feel useful and productive.

The barriers are still high against employing women in professions other than those traditionally associated with them, and many of the myths regarding women's ability to hold administrative and managerial positions still prevail. Illustrative of the inequalities women face when entering professional careers in business and industry are the difference in salaries offered to women as compared to those offered to men. A study by the Women's Bureau of the Department of Labor shows that, in six fields, women graduating from college in 1970 were being offered starting salaries from three to ten percent lower than those offered to men. Those statistics also show that, although the proportion of women among all workers increased between 1940 and 1969, women representing professional and technical workers decreased eight percent during the same period.

All women, including minister's wives, have society to content with—a society that prescribes roles for people and deviously points out that women's place is the home. In addition to relegating the woman to the role of housewife and mother, society prevents her from functioning independently and, therefore, hinders women establishing any identity. Rosalyn Baxandall clearly indicates this when she states that women never have a name. They first have their fathers' and then their husbands' name.

Men cannot understand women's discontent. After all, aren't they loved, honored, guarded, and cherished? They fail to realize that women do not want to live just through *them* and *their achievements* and their mutual offspring. Also, most men do not appreciate the fact that women do not enjoy the camaraderie of fellow workers as they do. A mind always in contact with children, whose aspirations and ambitions rise no higher than the roof that shelter it, is necessarily dwarfed in its proportions. It is understandable why women are so dissatisfied and couples grow apart, rather than closer, as years pass by. An article in *Ladies Home Journal* discussed a private detective agency's statistical study of runaway wives, which showed that 79.6% were in the 35-45 age bracket—and of this number, 75% were mothers running in hope of finding a life that would make them feel useful again. This certainly would emphasize the discontent of women, especially those who have lost their cloak of motherhood.

Women are raised in a manner that conditions them to accept a role which places them in a secondary position in relation to men. This dependence is not, as society would have us believe, based on woman's "natural" physical weakness or on an instinctive desire for dolls, or any other characteristic attributed to women as being "natural." Her dependence comes as a result of reacting to all the cultural pressures, implicit and explicit, which are brought to bear on her. The girl child is "programmed" for a passive role. She is taught that girls do not fight, and she is given dolls to play with. She is conditioned to being girlish by given frilly dresses to wear, which usually hamper robust physical activity. She is told to play with girls because boys are too rough. If a girl shows too much aggression or independence, she is encouraged to modify this behavior and to be more passive. Aggressiveness is reserved for males, in the family, and out of it.

Change is definitely needed because, although certain advertisers would have women believe they have come a long way, emancipation has not been fully achieved on any front. There are still glaring inequities in woman's economic, social, political, and legal standing. Perhaps more important from the psychological point of view, woman has not yet been able to free herself from discrimination against her own kind, from a feeling of inferiority.

It will take a great deal of effort to eradicate the idea of the inferior status of women because it is deeply rooted in society. Women, in their fight to change society's thinking must accept their plight as a common plight, see other women as reflections of themselves, and reject the faulty categories imposed on them by males for their own benefit.

Let me add that it takes a real man to appreciate and encourage his wife to enhance and complement his ministry in her area of talent or creativity. This is desirable so long as she knows her proper place in the church, and her achievements do not threaten her husband. It is the weak and insecure man who never encourages his wife, who keeps her in the background.

God's Divine Order certainly clears up this distorted outlook when Paul expresses his thoughts to the church in Ephesians. He said:

> So ought men to love their wives as their own bodies. He that loveth his wife loveth himself (Ephesians 5:28-29).

This is a beautiful insight because it deals with the similarity between the man's image of himself, and the parallel to his wife.

6

DIPLOMACY

The diplomat speaks and acts at the right time, in the best way and with the least offense. His motto is tact.

Not all Christians recognize the importance of speaking to one another without offending. True, there are those who are supersensitive, so that anything you say will be taken the wrong way. In light of these characteristics, the advantages are clearly defined in terms of its results.

As spiritual leaders, it is important that the attitudes of pastors and their wives reflect moderation and consistency in order to obtain the best results from those who seek counsel, instruction, or teaching. Many times a negative personality will hinder the work of the Lord.

Beverly LaHaye, asserts in her book, *The Spirit-Controlled Woman*: "Those weaknesses that hinder your relationship with Jesus Christ are a sin. Whenever you indulge in one weakness of your temperment, you can be sure that you will grieve or quench the Holy Spirit. This is a Sin." Although you try as best as you can to assist everyone spiritually, socially, or psychologically, you are not guaranteed success in all of your dealings. You are only an instrument used to admonish others through the medium of love. Through this process of love comes wisdom.

The fruit of the righteous is a tree of life; and he that

winneth souls is wise (Proverbs 11:30).

If wisdom is not projected in your efforts to win others to Christ, all of your time and exertion spent in preaching the gospel, will be in vain. Once you realize that the value of what you are saying, is weighed by how it is coming across, you will undoubtedly win more souls to Christ. You will pay attention to your attitude and try to develop charisma.

The pastor's wife must be sensitive to the feeling and needs of others so as not to offend those who seek her husband's help. It is, however, very important that the extent of sensitivity extended not intrude on her privacy barricade and break into her feminine needs. Jesus, our perfect example, was neither harsh nor rash in His dealings with the varied personalities with whom He came in contact. His main purpose and goal was to save souls through love. Our Lord's love in action and regard for mankind were unmistakably obvious.

The pastor's wife will be confronted with a mountain of circumstances which will demand that she be diplomatic in crucial situations. She will learn through experience that diplomacy is her strongest asset for success. There will be times in her life she will be misunderstood and even lied about. This is the time that she should stand firm on the truth, for truth will stand forever. Jesus said, "Love them that despitefully use you." And James said, "Let every man be swift to hear, slow to speak, slow to wrath" (James 1:19).

It seems so unfair that the feelings of others are considered to a greater degree than those of the pastor's wife. This is the price that a leader must pay to further the work of the Lord effectively. As his helpmate, she represents her husband in areas of his work when he is not available. There is never a clear-cut answer in resolving difficult situations within your local church, but the best procedure to use is diplomacy, finesse, and a keen sense of feeling for your brethren in the Lord.

I have been approached on one or two occasions with unpleasant remarks that were said about me. My first impulse was not necessarily the hurt by what was said; it was the content and triviality of what was said that was most damaging to me. A situation like this takes plenty of prayer to seek the mind of Christ. The worse accusation that can be made against you is that which is utterly false. This is not only damaging to the reputation of the pastor's wife, but to her husband's ministry. How does she deal with this situation? She doesn't. She tells the truth and leaves it alone. Truth, like cream always comes to the top. She lets the Lord fight her battles and in the process, God will maneauver good from bad, relegate bad from evil, and smooth out all of the rough edges (see Psalms 7:15).

In my particular case I finally realized it was best not to take matters into my own hands, but simply let the Lord work out each situation. He will always do a better job that we could ever do. What church members fail to recognize is that when they address themselves against their pastor's wife, they are in fact making accusations against their well loved pastor and against themselves. The apostle Paul clearly states in I Corinthians that we are the members of one body. When you speak against one member of the body of Christ, you are in essence speaking against yourself. This is the reason why some individuals find themselves year in and year out in the same predicament, never maturing in the Lord. This is because they are too busy finding fault with one another (ignorant of their own fault). They never learn the full meaning of the word *charity*, which is the greatest gift of the Spirit. Charity surpasses all the faith that could be given to man.

7

BROKEN RIBS

I was fascinated by an article in the *New York Daily News* regarding the clergyman's marriage breakup rate and the repercussions suffered by his ministry and the congregation. I was amazed to learn that the problems that exist among the ministerial couples are universal and surprisingly consistent throughout the church world. The number one complaint is that the minister's overcommitment to his church work causes a deficiency in the family life. There is also a build-up of resentment which, in most cases, never heals because it is never brought to the light. In addition, more wives are working and this causes conflict in the home. The congregation, on the other hand, resents that the minister's wife works; it feels she should direct all of her energies to church work. All of these nonscriptural excuses, are in most cases, personal convictions.

Many of the ministers interviewed for this article, emphasized their total commitment was to their congregation first. Another clergyman stated that, in his second marriage, he learned to be less committed to his work. This is an indication that he is lowering his standards to please his wife. In some instances, there can be an imbalance of one's priorities. As the minister gives himself to serve God and the congregation, it is quite natural that he will neglect his family to some extent. It will take an intelligent woman of God to slowly, surely, but gently, point out his family obligations and remind him that time and relaxation with the family, long overdue, will also do him a world of good.

The wife must learn to dole out her suggestions, criticisms, and point of view in small doses; this is more effective and conducive to his frame of mind. He will surprise you by thanking you for being so thoughtful and understanding. It is also the wife that provides, stimulates, and injects the "adhesive" quality needed to keep cohesive warmth flowing throughout the family unit. She must prod, explore, and create until she has found her solution.

Once upon a time, divorce among the clergy was frowned upon. Today, divorce has become a rather common occurrence, and results in spiritual, social, and economical disadvantages. Unresponsiveness to each other's problems and lack of communication in the home are America's greatest marriage killers. Sometimes just one (husband or wife) party's concerted effort will lead the other to catch hold of the existing problem. Many times it is the wife who must shoulder the responsibility of generating all of the patience that is necessary for the ultimate success of the ministry. She will eventually reap dividends if she can learn to wait. The problem exists when she becomes impatient, and loses out on her blessing.

An ex-wife faces the hazard of her status and identity being stripped; she can certainly look forward to hardships. However, if a pastor's wife looks harder at a difficult situation, trying to mend it and heal it and through the power of prayer, his ministry will grow and their marriage will have a deeper meaning. Most important, God will become the existence of their entire life. On the other hand, if marital problems cannot be solved, the pastor may believe he has lost his effectiveness in the pulpit and feels insecure in his role as a counselor; he could well wonder how he can help others when he cannot help himself.

There will always be those who will accept and condone anything the pastor sanctions. But may I add that I am not an advocate of double marriages.

34

What God has joined together, let no man put asunder
(Matthew 19:6).

8

EDUCATIONAL AND SOCIAL GOALS

Your dual relationship, education and social, should be proportioned evenly for a workable and balanced marriage. Though it is not essential and certainly not a prerequisite in determining the wife best suited for the pastor, it does help if both share the same social and educational status; this will help communication on an equal level.

Togetherness and unity are two closely related assets that add great strength and balance to a marriage. However, if for some reason the wife shows no interest in her husband's educational and social goals, there will undoubtedly develop a gulf of interest wide enough to cripple the marriage and damage his ministry. There cannot be unity without understanding, for this erases a multitude of doubts and discourages suspicion and insecurity. A workable marriage cannot be based on doubt, suspicion, or insecurity.

Lack of secular education does not necessarily mean you are uneducated. However, you can improve your social status by going to your local library and selecting reading material of value built around your home life, current events, and your husband's ministry. As most good books tend to increase learning capacity, they will make you an asset to your husband's ministry and at the same time offer personal enjoyment. You should also develop a friendly relationship with women of your ministerial setting; that could prove to be gratifying. Be sure you are discreet in your choice, for there are many such wives who have nothing spiritual or significant to offer but pure gossip. This is poor nutrition for a clean, saved life and will only produce an unproductive vessel which God cannot use.

I beseech you therefore, brethren, by the mercies of God, that ye present your bodies a living sacrifice, holy, acceptable unto God, which is your reasonable service (Romans 12:1).

Many times, one's economic status or family structure can impede and immobilize you making it difficult to achieve the desired goals. In time, God makes a way for you to obtain a new venture. Bible School or Sunday School workshops should be first and foremost in selecting your priorities. Fundamental Bible courses, Bible doctrine, Sunday School techniques, and any other course that will help you understand your husband's ministry should be seriously considered. Your role as the pastor's wife should be a positive one. It is always easier to give up than to persist in the midst of adversity when trying to achieve such goals. Life, with its many complexities, adversities, and uncertainties, makes it crucially important that you consult God in every decision made; only Christ affords a sure, secure, and firm foundation.

For other foundation can no man lay than that which is laid, which is Jesus Christ (I Corinthians 3:11).

Remember that when everything else fails, God never fails. When you submit your will to God, you automatically dispel doubt from your way of life and strengthen your faith that God is going to make everything all right. God desires that we walk by faith and not by sight (see 2 Corinthians 5:17).

When you fail to show interest in each other's social and intellectual interests, you create a gap in your communication and cause undue conflict in the work of the ministry. Seek to excel in an area built around your personality. Work at it, enhance it until it engulfs and fills your needs. This will ultimately give you that life you have been longing for. Most important, gear *all* of your energies towards pleasing God.

The size and social structure of your church membership will determine how extensive you will need to project your ability as a hostess. As the pastor's wife, you must realize that being a hostess covers various areas. Many times your efforts toward showing the proper manners, assembling the proper attire and creating the proper atmosphere can easily be exaggerated and overemphasized to the extent of failure. Trying too hard will ofttimes prove to be the negative approach.

My basic recipe for the essential ingredients and the right temperature for your role in hostessing is met by these six (6) easy steps:

1. Be natural and be yourself, for you have a unique personality that makes you who you are.
2. Be friendly and kind; try to generate warmth.
3. Gear your catering expertise to all age groups within your church. If you fail the first time, try again. Each church membership consists of an average of four or five generations; it therefore becomes necessary to learn the art of "loving" young and old.
4. Your ministry, entails not only the greeting with the ready smile, and standing by your husband's side, but it covers sick beds, problem situations, cleaning homes when needed, counseling, and whatever your hands find to do. Be sure to do all in Jesus' name and with all your might.
5. Never feel that you've "got it made", for it is a constant learning experience just dealing with people of all classes.
6. Try to attune the luxury of your sensitivity to the sensitivity of others.

Be kindly affectioned one to another with brotherly love; in honour preferring one another (Romans 12:10).

38

Purchase a book on etiquette to point out areas of crucial importance; it will prove to be a great source of enlightenment. A cook book is also good to have on hand because you never know when you might serve angels unaware. Being a good cook, a good hostess, a good conversationalist, and projecting prudence (exercising sound judgement) complement and enhance your husband's ministry.

Don't try to impress the members with an extravagant house, but make it livable, comfortable, and perfumed with warmth. Paul encourages us to practice hospitality in our worship to God: "Distributing to the necessity of saints; given to hospitality" (Romans 12:13).

When your husband begins to climb the ladder of success, you must be prepared to avail yourself socially, intellectually, and most important, spiritually. It is incumbent upon you to be equipped in all of the above areas and to be ready for his height of success in Christ. Prepare yourself for the success. First, be aware that your husband's ministry may grow by leaps and bounds. Secondly, don't harbor a negative attitude, but be completely positive in order to stimulate a pleasant ambiance between you and your husband. Third, ask God's direction in organizing your priorities so as to grow into the type of pastor's wife that God desires. Surprisingly, you will find yourself completely engulfed in many areas that you never planned or imagined you would be a part of. But because of your initial groundwork, you will find you are now on your way towards a stimulating, challenging, exciting and invigorating work for the Master.

9

PERSONAL EXPERIENCES

You must be able to cope with existing problems at any given time. Crisis and conflicts should be dealt with on a day-to-day basis. Problems can arise so sporadically, that you must be prepared and cushioned "well" in advance for any and everything to break loose; either that or you could go insane. Don't anticipate or plan for problems ahead of time but plan for your emotional strength.

Dr. Marion H. Nelson, Christian psychiatrist and author stated that "Being a pastor's wife is the most hazardous and dangerous occupation a woman can have." He believes that only the best emotionally adjusted—those who have had deep love and security in childhood, and who are thick-skinned—will ever come through the experience emotionally and mentally unscarred. It may sound comical, but this is a fact. Many times before we eventually and completely "trust in God," we are faced with developing a system of organizing our priorities. If our problems are to keep balance, our priorities must maintain an equilibrium.

The apostle Paul tells us so beautifully in Timothy 1:7 that God has not given us the spirit of fear, but of power, love and of a sound mind. God gives us the capabilities, the ingenuity and wisdom to work out our everyday problems.

My husband and I had the privilege in the infancy of his

40

ministry to endure much suffering for the cause of Christ. I think back and ponder how we overcame, but God maneuvered on our behalf. His ultimate plan was to mold and make us vessels for his honor and glorification. I personally feel that a minister and his wife are at a great disadvantage without experiences of suffering for the cause of Christ. Being able to relate to others who are going through circumstances is meaningful and encouraging to others at such a time.

I can remember so vividly the first year we were married. Things were pretty rough. We would always console each other with these words: "Things will get better, they can't get any worse." And believe me, they got worse! At the time, I had only one black suit that I was able to get into, having gained a little weight. It was a blessing that when I was single, I bought expensive clothing. In spite of the weight gain, which made it impossible to wear all of my clothes, one particular knit suit, surprisingly enough, stretched so that it was never too tight, nor did it cling. That was certainly the handiwork of God. Everywhere I went, the suit went. Accenting it were many different accessories: a scarf, a necklace, a blouse underneath or a sweater, and sometimes, just a simple gold pin. Many times I was embarrassed, especially when everyone told me how well I looked. I suppose I doubted their sincerity because it was the same group of people we saw at the various meetings. It was certainly an indication to me that God was blessing in the form of a "suit." Many times we look for God to bless us in one way and He blesses in a completely different manner.

The Lord blessed me on another occasion when a cousin and a dear friend both lost weight; fortunately, I stayed my healthy robust self and reaped beautiful dresses, suits, coats and shoes. Surprisingly, they looked brand new. I was not above receiving second-hand clothes; I considered them as blessings in disguise. People many times ridicule the pastor's wife because she is either too stylish or not stylish enough. What is unfortunate is that many times things you have gone through for the cause of Christ are not known by others (and

41

should be known only by God and the person concerned). When God decides to bless you, he determines how expensive your blessings will be. I've found this out myself, buying new apparel when the Lord blessed, and not wearing it for about a month. I did not want to give the appearance of prosperity and abundance, because so many feel *poverty* and *salvation* go together. I have learned that when God decides to bless you materially, we should not inhibit blessings, but rather accept them.

In the book, *The Pastor's Wife and the Church* by Dorothy Harrison Pentecost, I read a passage of the deacon's prayer: "Lord, you keep him (the pastor) humble; we'll keep him poor." Many times, folk are happy with the pastor's wife just so long as she's plain, simple, and unassuming.

By recognizing these tendencies within the church and being aware that they do exist, you can better handle and understand each given situation with the help of the Lord; not knowing what to expect can be the problem. I've found serving God to be one great big adventure: one excitement after another. Our prayer should always be, "Lord, don't move that mountain, but give me grace to overcome." Many times we pester God not for his perfect will in our lives, but for what we think we need, not realizing that what we think we need is not always what God wants us to have. Ultimately, God removes the problem out of His permissive will and we miss out on the fulfilling blessing. Conquering the problem would be far greater than going through life with one weak testimony after another, or with no real meaning and purpose to our ultimate goal—to see Jesus one day.

Being a pastor's wife puts many restrictions on you within the congregation. Regardless of how large or how small the membership, demands are made either openly or by suggestion. An average church spans about three to four generations. Each generation has its standards, ideas, restrictions based on background, many of which were placed upon them years ago. Each segment feels you should live up to its standard; whether you do or not is of no consequence. You also have members who transfer from other churches with independent ideas. They do not realize they subconsciously transfer the patterns of their pastor's wife to you.

There are many who have a pattern called "the model pastor's wife," which is unscriptural and man-made. This man-made model is generally a stereotype. People, however, feel that her attire, hair style, and general appearance should be matronly, simple, and that she should never draw attention to herself. Everyone has different concepts and interpretations of the proper attire that God requires for the minister's wife, and in many cases, the problems arise because people are still living in the past. The word of God speaks of the woman's dress as modest. However, there are many concepts of the word "modesty." Webster's dictionary says: "freedom from conceit or vanity; propriety in dress, speech or conduct." Many times people place emphasis on colors: red, orange, pink versus black, brown, gray. This limited view regarding modesty causes undue conflict that a minister's wife must be aware of. Her remedy is, prayer, diplomacy and plenty of *love*. There can never be a set model or set standard, only what God requires. Man looks on the outward appearance but God looks on the heart. Joel 2:13 says: "Rend your heart, and not your garment." The apostle Paul speaks in Corinthians about dressing in modesty. We find that in order to get the significant meaning of each scripture, we must rightly divide the Word of truth (see I Tim. 2:15). Although every member has certain expectations and requirements for you as a pastor's wife, live up to the complete expectations of God and your husband as best you can. Insurmountable problems develop, when, in an effort to please everyone, you please no one, not even God. As a pastor's wife, you should never exhibit qualities in your personality that might be a permanent detriment to your husband's ministry. What you must understand is that you are only the pastor's wife. The pastor is the one whom the members regard as their "savior." He is the one they can come to for advice, strength, and encouragement. Many times, one hasty word or an impulsive remark made by you will follow you to your grave. Although God forgives and forgets, the members will forgive but will never forget. Therefore, you are labeled as a troublemaker, bossy in nature, and unmatched for their well-loved pastor. Uncanny as it might seem, some feel that they would make a better wife than you for their pastor. Many times, unconsciously, they develop a father-image of him, which may further develop into the deeper emotional attachment, "love." When you see these tendencies existing in your local church, ask God for guidance. Don't take anything into your hands without first consulting God. Begin to pray, not for yourself, but for her, that God will begin to build her spiritual priorities in God, to make her a better person for the all-around good. And as God begins to help her, you will unknowingly develop a special love in your heart for her. When you begin to have problems, seek God first. You might also seek another pastor's wife with more experience and one who is known for her meekness, love, and prayerful life. Seek a person on that order for spiritual advice and guidance, not a busybody or someone that is known for gossip.

On the basis of my personal experience in dealing with various situations, I have learned to completely depend on the Lord to receive my main source of strength in the time of need. There are times, however, when we all need that human touch of understanding which is expressed and shared by one another through the love; a source to encourage, strengthen and admonish.

The Lord blessed me with a "dear" saint of God whose name I dear not mention for fear of offending others who are equally as special to me. Her quiet, sweet spirit is like a tower of strength, that gives me the encouragement that I need— even if it is just her ear. Most significantly, her advice is always spiritually and prayerfully directed, and her method of application is "Charity." This rare quality (charity) is esteemed higher than any spiritual gift and supersedes the greatest degree of faith (I Corinthians 13:1-5). This is an indication of the power of love—given only through our Lord Jesus Christ. I have learned, however, through my experiences that there are many psuedonyms used for love among the people of God:

1. Selfish Love—Self interest: have no time for others or either preoccupied by your own selfish concern.
2. Limited Love—Restricted: "I will accommodate you today, but tomorrow is out of the question."
3. Conditioned Love—The "if, then" theory: "If you love me, then I will love you."

You will never realize your greatest potential if you manifest any of the loves cited above. God who is rich in mercy is able to give you the abundance of love needed to influence other individuals in "ALL" walks of life (see Ephesians 2:4). This is my prayer each day:

Lord, help me to be a blessing to someone in need—spiritually, psychologically, socially, financially, and in whatever capacity. Lord, help me to apply and season my efforts with *Your* love and abundance of grace. Lord, finally but most important, help me *never* to remind others that I have been a blessing to them. I am not the blessing giver, you are; I am just an instrument, a vessel used for your glory.

10

QUESTIONS ASKED BY MINISTERS' WIVES

I have compiled a list of questions that were most frequently asked by ministers' wives and students at my local seminar; the answers given are also listed.

Q. My husband started showing jealous tendencies after I became interested in furthering my education. As a man of God, should he project this jealousy towards me?

A. For any marriage to be workable, there must be togetherness, not only spiritual, but social and educational. God has a divine order for the people of God, but society has enmeshed the minds of some to exhibit a movement of new liberality for women. Society does in fact make impressions on your lives; the important key to remember is not to let it direct your life, or channel it out the will of God.

There is nothing wrong, when you decide to finish your education as long as God is pleased with your motives. Your education can ultimately be an asset to your husband's ministry. Don't try to surpass his educational realm as this will definitely cause conflicts.

Your husband is obviously exhibiting a latent tendency that can be corrected if dealt with properly. As the wife, don't assume the "know it all!" attitude. Take your new learning experience in stride; ask his advice and make him feel very much needed.

As Proverbs 4:7 says, "In all your getting, get understanding." Don't aggravate the situation by discussing your studies morning, noon and night. On the contrary, encourage his interest in your conversation and stimulate an awareness that, whatever his interest, you respect and value his ideas. In time, his jealousy will become minimal, and you will see the birth of a new man right before your eyes.

Q. How should a young wife behave when her husband reveals that he is called to the ministry?

A. The reactions to his new-found calling can be various, depending upon her personality. Many times the wife discerns that God is leading her husband in a special and different way. If, however, her husband's calling is in fact a complete surprise and upsets her, she will have to show an initial, genuine effort to understand. Conflict will arise for both involved when seeking the mind of Christ as a minister; he tries to please God and also tries to please a wife who verbalizes her discontent and projects unhappiness. If this presents a problem in your life, seek a qualified man of God (your pastor or a counselor). Don't wait until things have gotten out of hand. Try to deal with your problems a day at a time and let prayer be your guide in all situations.

Q. Is it beneficial to the pastor if he discusses the members' problem, traits, etc., with his wife?

A. The wife of a minister plays many roles; she develops these positions quite often out of necessity. In the sight of God, the two (husband and wife) are one. However, relating various problems and information to some wives can be a disaster. The wife should augment her husband's ministry by exhibiting the following characteristics: integrity; prudence; and trust.

Q. When members call your husband and he is not at home,

should you encourage them to reveal the nature of the call to you?

A. State that you will take the message. If they care to discuss the nature of their call with you, give them the opportunity to suggest it on their own. There are some who will confide in you as their pastor's wife but be very sure that the information is kept in strict confidence. On the other hand, there will be those who feel only the pastor understands and cares for them. Don't feel personally offended. Recognize that your role should project a pleasant warm, feeling to the members not only in person but also over the phone.

Q. What can the minister's wife do to help her husband to develop his fullest potential?

A. The minister's wife is the key to her husband's success; the extent of how far he will excel depends upon her interest and her desire for him to achieve. She is the determining factor in programming his chances to reach his fullest potential. Unless she shares in his ideas, hopes, desires, and dreams to accomplish God's will, she can be a discouraging factor. Instead of being a blessing to his ministry, she will erect a platform for constant battle. The pastor's wife should:

1. Learn how to encourage her husband even when she needs encouragement herself.
2. Never compare her husband to another minister.
3. Never publicly criticize her husband; it will destroy his self-confidence.
4. Be loving and understanding.
5. Share her husband's accomplishments with enthusiasm.
6. Reassure him when he feels inadequate.
7. Increase his confidence by "admiring him," it won't hurt.
8. Make the children aware that dad is the authority in the home; she is the only one that can initiate that awareness.

9. Never criticize her husband in front of the children, especially when he is disciplining them. Wait until she and hubby are alone to disagree.
10. Compliment her husband on his wisdom, and be objective in criticism.

Q. Should the pastor's wife have close personal friends in the church?

A. She should never develop close friends within the church her husband pastors because of so many adverse repercussions that could develop. She should be warm and friendly to all, but not intimate or show partiality. It becomes very difficult to become intimate with church members and at the same time maintain respect. If she had already established a close relationship with someone long before she was placed in this role, that would be an exception to the rule.

Q. What should you do when the pastor's wife is young and the older members find it difficult giving her respect?

A. It will take an initial effort on her part as a young wife to earn respect.

1. Be positive about everything you do.
2. Give the mature members their due respect and in time yours will come. The "key" to remember is learning how to wait.
3. Respect their life experience.
4. Be warm and affectionate. Love them and they in time will love you.

Q. As the pastor's wife, should I serve and participate in every auxiliary in my church?

A. The pastor's wife should show a general interest in all auxiliaries. Once you focus your interest on one auxiliary and not on others, you give the appearance of showing partiality. Be able to spread yourself evenly, yet effectively.

Q. What fruits or gifts should I desire as a pastor's wife to be a blessing to my husband's ministry?

A. All fruits of the Spirit (Galatians 5:22) should be in the life of every spirit-filled believer. However, if there is a gift that you desire, ask God in faith to use you, and I promise He will supply all of your needs according to His will in your life.

Q. How should I as a pastor's wife behave when my husband takes out all of his frustration on me?

A. Since you recognize that your husband is taking his frustrations out on you, although you are not the cause, look beyond his sharpness and respond with understanding and gentleness. In time he will return with an apology. He will also recognize that he was unjust in using you as a scapegoat. Forgive him, love him and understand. In time, he will outgrow that stage and will love you the more for your patience and understanding.

Q. How should I occupy my time when my husband is seldom home? Being aware of my husband's role in serving the people, I find an emptiness on my part when I feel unfulfilled.

A. Ask God for something that gives you fulfillment. Be able to work independently and interdependently in effectively administering to the people and to your husband. You have your own ministry, use it. While your husband is being fulfilled, you can also get your fulfillment in your area of expertise.

Q. Why should I, the wife of a minister, be required to sacrifice and suffer for the ministry when God called him and not me?

A. The wife of a pastor cannot exempt or separate herself from the many trials and tests associated with the pastorate, because of her close relationship to the man that God ordained. Neither can she receive the rewards and blessings associated with the pastorate unless she has sacrificed and shed briny tears along with her husband. True your husband was called and not you, but being the wife of a minister puts you in a spiritual realm

50

that forces you to be sensitive to the ministry. The fact that you are his helpmate is "God ordained" (Genesis 2:18), and allows you to be an instrument. Your type of acceptance will determine how effective your husband's ministry will be. When you and your husband were joined together in holy matrimony (a holy act) you became one. When God called your husband to the ministry (another holy act), you were also included in the calling. If your attitude towards the ministry is a positive one, then he has a 75% chance to succeed; the other 25% chance of failure or effectiveness is beyond your efforts. There is a true expression that says, "A woman can either break or make a man." I would like to add to that another profound statement: "But if that man is truly *not* a man, not even the greatest woman in the world can make him the man that never was."

11

EPILOGUE

The Pastor's Rib and His Flock was written to share, and hope-fully, encourage, other ministers' wives throughout the world as they go through the struggles, anticipations, burdens, and joys associated with this unique role. Second, it was written to stimulate the minds of the parishioners who might not have had the opportunity to objectively perceive the many roles their "first lady" must assume. There are demands that are placed on the pastor's wife by the members, the society, and even herself. In light of this struggle, she must make sure that God is pleased with her motives and objectives by ascer-taining the perfect will of God. The members, however, can make a significant contribution to the minister's wife, simply with a kind word, a kind deed, or a kind act. You will be sur-prised to know that she needs encouragement just like ev-eryone else.

My concern is also directed to the potential minister's wife who may have erroneous and romantic ideas of what she feels her life will be like. It is so much easier to adjust to a situation when made aware of experiences of others. Ministers are trained through college and seminaries for the task of dealing with people, places, and personalities. They are in-structed in psychology, sociology, philosophy, theology, and good old "kneeology." My concern, however, is that before the pastor can be fruitful and successful, his wife must be equipped with some basic knowledge and understanding to prepare her emotionally, and to give her some insight into what is in store for her.

Based on my experience of the past fourteen years, I must say I have gained spiritual enrichment, a deeper devotion to my brothers and sisters, and the most significant realization that I share in the greatest occupation of all.

APPENDIX

THE PASTOR'S RIB AND HIS FLOCK

A Teaching Guide for a Seminar for Pastors' and Ministers' Wives

INTRODUCTION

This seminar is designed to be taught from 12 to 14 weeks per semester, one night each week, and 1½ hours per session.

Prerequisite: Students "must" be married to a minister.

Aims: To prepare each student spiritually (most important), emotionally, and psychologically to aid her husband and his ministry; to know the importance of her place as a minister's wife; and to excel to whatever height God designs for her. To deal with issues relevant to a young wife of a pastor:

—Age limitations;
—Personal convictions vs. biblical and scriptural restrictions;
—Individuality—to be your real self (don't pattern yourself after man-made MODELS). To stimulate in each minister's wife, a deep sense of identity, and to create involvement among all women.

55

Procedures: Be sure to give each student equal time to participate. Begin each session with prayer for God's guidance and approval. Develop a very informal and relaxed atmosphere. Share views and ideas for edification and to create a close relationship among students. Stress punctuality.

LESSON I

Have students fill out a 3x5 card giving name, address, home phone, business phone; state whether a minister or a pastor's wife. This has a *threefold purpose*: to be able to contact students in case of unanticipated absence or changes in class schedule; to compile a class roster and mailing list; and to give you some idea of the scope to cover and the need to distinguish between the role of the minister's wife and that of the pastor's wife.

Give each student a syllabus outlining what to expect for the entire term. Include a calendar for the semester.

Ask what each hopes to gain from this course; ask for problems for discussion. Emphasize that each student will get out only what he puts into the course.

If possible, seat students in a circle for informality; have each person introduce herself and give a brief synopsis of her church affiliation. This will eliminate tension among students and will create a family atmosphere.

Finally, state your credentials: Your education, how long you have been a pastor's wife, and a testimony revealing experiences as a pastor's wife.

Then discuss the aim, theme, and motto of the lesson.

Aim: To make sure students feel comfortable and at ease with you as their instructor. It is also important that they feel you have first-hand experience as a pastor's wife.

Theme: "My little children, let us not *love* in word, neither in tongue; but in deed and in truth (I John 3:18).

Motto: Wait on the Lord: be of good courage, and He shall strengthen thine heart: *Wait,* I say, on the Lord.

Discuss briefly books (all published by Moody Press) you

56

will use during the entire semester:

The Pastor's Wife and the Church, by Dorothy Harrison
Pentecost

The Unprivate Life of a Pastor's Wife, by Frances Nordland

The Christian Home In a Changing World, by Gene Getz

Have students read *The Pastor's Wife and the Church*
throughout the entire semester. There will be a short question
period after each session on this book.

LESSON 2
CAUSE AND EFFECT

Aim: To be prepared spiritually, psychologically, and emotionally for the role of minister's wife. To point out the distinction
between the young wife and the mature wife.

Limitations:
1. What God expects of you (see Romans 12:1);
2. Your responsibility to your husband (see I Corinthians
11:3);
3. What is expected of you from church members and
society (non-scriptural).

List cause and effect:
— financial insolvency
— sensitive and vulnerable to hurt feelings
— inexperienced and often impetuous
— discuss

Needs: Develop a one-to-one relationship with God and ask
for direction, then wait patiently for His answer.

LESSON 3
ASSETS AND LIABILITIES

Aims: To discuss, in depth, attitudes that can indeed affect
your husbands' ministry, spiritually, emotionally and

psychologically. To get students to recognize their own deficiencies. By observing their own insufficiencies, they can better help others. To identify assets and liabilities; strong points versus weak points.

ASSETS   LIABILITIES

Get the class to participate and list assets and liabilities.

Write on the board the qualities that can affect a pastor's ministry.

Ask the question: "How can *you* improve each negative action displayed on your part?" Give the scriptures listed below as a "remedy" for each of the following negative actions:

1. Argumentative   —Galatians   5:26
2. Bossy   —Galatians   5:22 (Gentleness)
3. Sensitive   —Acts 20:35
4. Pessimistic   —Romans 14:23
5. Perfectionist   —Galatians   5:22 (longsuffering)
6. Unthankful   —2 Timothy   3:2
                    —St. Luke   6:35

Assignment: Give out Priority Sheets to hand in for next class. Make sure *all* answers are defended scripturally.

LESSON 4
PROBLEMS VS. PRIORITIES—PART I

Aim: To prepare students to deal with their family responsibilities in keeping each situation in perspective: husband; children; home.

Thought: "Don't let your good be evil spoken of" (Romans 14:16).

Assignment: Read *The Christian Home in a Changing World,* chapters 3,4, and 10.

58

Discuss how to establish a well balanced life in God that every pastor's wife should desire. Ask if any one has experienced any problem regarding family responsibilities and divided balances.

LESSON 5
PROBLEMS VS. PRIORITIES—PART 2

Aim: To reinforce God's divine order in the minds of the participants.

Thought: As the body needs a well balanced diet, so does the spiritual man.

Conduct group discussion and Interaction regarding situations that are relevant. Examples:

— Husband and wife working
— Continuation of education
— Children/social life
— Housework/soap operas

Assignment: Have students read *The Unprivate Life of the Pastor's Wife,* chapters 11 and 12, to finalize thoughts on "priority."

LESSON 6
HOW TO DEVELOP A DEEPER SENSE OF SPIRITUAL AWARENESS

Aims: To establish the means to spiritual awareness, which are:

1. Prayer
2. Bible study
3. Fasting

To establish the significance of fasting:
1. Sacrifice

2. To develop personal discipline
The more you pray, the less you think of yourself.

Operational Definition: To be sensitive and responsive to the moving, directions, works and the will of God.

Spirit Indwelling: Ezek. 36:27; John 14:17; Romans 8:9; I Cor. 6:19, 20; I John 2:27

Process of Development: Romans 5:1-5

Spiritual Verification: Romans 8:16; Gal. 4:6; I John 3:24; 1 John 4:13

LESSON 7
YOUR ATTITUDES: NEGATIVE OR POSITIVE

Aims: To stress the importance of maintaining a positive attitude with their husbands, i.e.:

- —increasing his self-confidence with love and understanding.
- —encouraging even when you need encouragement.
- —sharing his accomplishments with enthusiasm.
- —reassuring him when he feels insecure.

Ask the question: "How do you think these gestures will strengthen his ministry?" Have students answer the question on paper and hand in at end of class.

LESSON 8
WHOM DID GOD CALL:
YOU OR YOUR HUSBAND?

Aims: To establish to the wives, their vocation and status as a minister's wife.

Emphasize that God called their husbands, not them; however, they can be a great asset and influence in his success. Their position, as the pastor's wife, can either help or hinder.

Ask for examples—either personal testimonies or hypothetical. Students should be aware that they are the determining factor to his height of success or failure in the ministry. If the wife engenders a subtle tenderness instead of an obvious shove, his ministry will lead to ultimate success.

Ask for suggestions and ideas to use in aiding their husbands.

LESSON 9
NEEDS

Aims: To stress the importance of wives receiving their own *fulfillment,* independent of their husbands.

To create an excitement in whatever makes them happy, all subject to the will of God.

Conduct group discussion of:

—Volunteer work
—Prayer ministry
—Sewing for others
—Creative writing
—Teaching small groups within the local church
—Helping teenagers
—Being a better mother

Emphasize the tremendous ministry of drawing others to Christ.

If wives have no fulfillment, their experience will be meaningless. They will become frustrated and an ultimate liability to their husband's life.

LESSON 10
CHANGE

Aim: To project to the minister's wife, the member concept regarding "the model pastor's wife."
Thought: "Change is inevitable."

Encourage participants to make sure their motives are spiritual and sincere.

Ask students to list personal convictions.

Discuss man-made models and scriptural validity.

List the ten (10) attributes.

LESSON 11
EDUCATIONAL AND SOCIAL GOALS

Aim: To stress the importance of having a cohesive relationship, both educationally and socially.
Thought: When this happy medium exists, you create a well rounded relationship.

Become interested in whatever makes your husband happy. Don't be too critical of his friends even if you don't particularly like them. Lavish him with plenty of *TLC*.

Inevitably he will come around and do the things that you *like*.

Have a three-group discussion on:

1. Educational conflict
2. Social conflict

LESSON 12
YOUR BODY IS NOT YOUR OWN

Aim: To establish the importance of well balanced meals and diets that will not hamper the work of God.
Thought: Many times we eat in excess and the body becomes unfit for God's army.

Ask for examples relating to everyday situations.

Restricted diets
High blood pressure
Diabetes
Obesity
- Pork
- Sweets
- Soda

Scripture:
"What? Know ye not that your body is the temple of the Holy Ghost which is in you, which ye have of God, and ye are not your own?
"For ye are bought with a price: Therefore glorify God in your body, and in your spirit, which are God's" (I Cor. 6:19-20).

LESSON 13
YOUR CHILDREN—PART I

Aim: To provide children with their basic needs, such as:

Family Devotion	—Be sure to set a scheduled time for each gathering.
Family Recreation	—Develop some type of recreation that the family can enjoy together.
Family Council	—Build a parent/child relationship, respect views, whether or not you believe them.
	It becomes quite important to the child that you listen and not criticize.

Assignment: Read, *Heaven Help the Home*, Pages 15-25.
To be discussed during next class:
—The foundation of the home and the total existence for the Christian home.
—Psalm 127.

—Children must be cultivated like a flower in order to bloom into fruits of labor.

LESSON 14
YOUR CHILDREN—PART 2

Reference: Heaven Help the Home, pages 15-25.
Aim: To establish parent's responsibility to their *children.*

Discuss the foundation of the home and the total existence for the Christian Home.

Emphasize that children must be cultivated like a flower in order to bloom into fruits of labor.

Discuss topic on page 10: "Society Depends on the Family."

Reach a solution from class participation.

LESSON 15
ROLE CONFLICT

Aim: To establish the existence of role conflict with the ministerial couple.

Reasons:
—The need to satisfy the wife's fulfillment.
—Forced to work to compensate their husband's salary and make ends meet.

Conflict arises due to the following:
—When as a minister's wife, she fails to produce spiritually and hinders the work of God.
—When her motives are not in accordance with God's will.
—When the family is neglected.
—When she can no longer share in his ministry because of her job responsibilities.
—When she fails to produce as a wife to her husband.

Scripture:
  I Peter 3:1
  I Corinthians 11:3
  I Corinthians 7:3-4
  Ephesians 5:28-29

FINAL REMARKS AND IMPLEMENTATION

If for some reason, you have completed this course before the twelve-week period, you can implement your class by using one of the techniques listed below.

1. Teaching through role playing. Students test several solutions to very realistic problems and the application is immediate.
2. Bring in films related to class material. Discuss film.
3. Have guest speakers
   —pastor's wives
   —ministers' wives
   —Psychologists
   —Educators
4. Buzz Groups—Divide class into six-member clusters; ask each to discuss a certain problem for six minutes.
5. Panel Discussion—Allow one hour class period: ten minutes for introduction of panel members, and thirty minutes for the presentation. Then . . .
6. Questions and Answers—Question and answer teaching gives the student the opportunity to reflect on her inquiries and ascertain needs for his further guidance

TEACHING MATERIALS FOR A SEMINAR
FOR PASTORS' AND MINISTERS' WIVES

I. Give an appraisal of your true-self, listing *only* the *"negative"* side of your personality that can affect your husbands' ministry.

   A. *Purpose:* to correct your deficiencies in aiding your development and spiritual growth. By getting rid of your negative attributes, you strengthen your husbands' ministry.

KEEP AN UP-TO-DATE PROGRESS REPORT OF YOUR DEVELOPMENT

Be objective   * PROGRESS CODES
Be truthful

Name:

Starting date:

Problem areas

	Jan.	Feb.	Mar.	Apr.	May	June	July	Aug	Sept.	Oct.	Nov.	Dec
1.												
2.												
3.												
4.												
5.												
6.												
7.												
8.												
9.												
10.												

* 1. Making a genuine effort   2. Improving   3. Becoming more consistent
* 4. He sees the change   5. Our relationship has changed for the good

II. *GIVE AN APPRAISAL OF EACH INVITED GUEST (MINISTERS' WIVES)*
  A. Was her talk relevant?   Discuss.
  B. Did you enjoy her?   Why.
  C. What impressed you most?
  D. Would you categorize her as the *"model pastors' wife?"* Discuss.
  E. In her presentation, did she generate a part in her personality that you feel is an asset? And what did you admire in her personality?

III. *PRIORITIES*

In your role as a minister's wife, your responsibility and devotion requires your attention in *all* areas listed below.
Please list in order as you know God would have it to be.
Defend your decisions *scripturally* and *doctrinally.*

Put in
correct order

1) Home
2) Hobbies
3) Children
4) Worship to God
5) Total commitment to God
6) Commitment to your husband
7) Church participation
8) Preparing well-balanced meals
9) Rest/relaxation
10) Giving yourself attention

_____
_____
_____
_____
_____
_____
_____
_____
_____
_____

III. *PRIORITIES* (completed, with relevant scriptural references added)
In your role as a minister's wife, your responsibility and devotion requires your attention in *all* areas listed below.
Please list in order as you know God would have it to be.
Defend your decisions *scripturally* and *doctrinally.*

PUT IN
CORRECT ORDER

1)	Home	5
2)	Hobbies	4
3)	Children	6
4)	Worship to God	3
5)	Total commitment to God	1
6)	Commitment to your husband	8
7)	Church participation	7
8)	Preparing well-balanced meals	9
9)	Rest/relaxation	10
10)	Giving yourself attention	2

5) Rom. 12:1 II Tim. 2:15 1 Cor. 11:3
4) Rom. 12:1
6) 1 Cor. 11:3 1 Cor. 11:8-9
    Eph. 5:21-33 (submit) 1 Cor. 7:3-5 Col. 3:18
3) Eph. 5:23 *Titus 2:4 1 Tim. 3:4-5
1) Titus 2:4-5
8) Titus 2:4-5
7) Heb. 10:25
9) Mark 6:31
10) Rom. 12:10 Rom. 14:19 Rom. 14:1 Rom. 15
2) ---